The Language of Spirituality

Alan York

*To my wife, Pauline, for her inspiration and encouragement,
and for her enduring patience with me.*

Acknowledgements

I would like to thank Britain's Yearly Meeting of the Religious Society of Friends for its continual support for Quaker religious life in Britain (including mine), and the Universalist Group of British Quakers, and especially its clerk, Tony Philpott, for particular help, advice, and support over numbers of years.

Contents

Part Two: Mind, Brain, and Spirit

Introduction

This book attempts to make sense of religion and spirituality for 21st century people. We will look at the relationship between the two, and after the Prelude (a boy's experience of growing up with religion), we examine, in Part One, the role of religious language, contrasting this with that of scientific language, and concluding that it is human experience, in all its forms, that is central to any valid notion of spirituality.

In Part Two, after the Interlude on Graven Images, we look in some detail at a 21st century attempt to account for the human mind and hence, perhaps, for spirituality, in scientific terms, using Quantum Mechanics and Relativity as the means.

Our conclusions are open-ended, but we hope to allow for a new intellectual frame for spirituality, which is something our present century demands.

Prelude

The small boy sat in his pew with his big brother and his mom and dad, listening to the Lay Reader expounding the Anglican view of things.

For the boy, the world of which the Lay Reader spoke was as real as the seat he sat on; Jesus, Son of God, had come to Earth 1946 years before and saved everyone in some way. We owed Jesus everything: Angels and Archangels had told the world about Him, and God the Father was seated in Heaven with Jesus by his side.

Above the boy's head on the wall of the small church was a statuette of Jesus on the cross.

The boy didn't understand about the cross, but he could see Jesus alright, close by him, made of some chocolate-coloured stuff. In fact, he imagined that the Jesus he could see there was actually made of chocolate – a delicacy he had only recently come across after the war. Perhaps, he imagined a bit later, this chocolate Jesus was the reason people talk about "sweet Jesus."

He knew the story of the stable, Mary and Joseph, the shepherds and the wise men, all gathered around the baby Jesus, and he knew that it was all something true and wonderful.

His schoolteacher said so. The parish Rector agreed with the Lay Reader, and they were all, like his mom and dad, clearly in awe of the whole thing.

The boy grew older, went to the little church regularly, and said five prayers, at his mom's instruction, every night before sleep.

His big brother was already in the church choir, and, indeed, the Boys' Brigade with its heady mixture of bands, church parades, football, and camping. After a time, the boy himself and his friends all joined the "BB," and some went on with the boy in joining the choir, with choir practice during the week and church eventually three times every Sunday. There was Evensong and Sermon, conducted by the Lay Reader when the boy and some of his friends were in the choir stalls singing psalms, responses, and hymns. There was Sunday School, when various ladies tried to teach the boys catechistic things, and exciting Sunday School day trips to Barmouth, Porthcawl and Cheddar Gorge.

The other significant Sunday event, however, was Holy Communion at 9.00 am, conducted by the much revered, friendly, and loving Rector, who came weekly to this small daughter church from the centre of the parish two miles away to conduct the mysterious and holy ceremonies of the Eucharist.

People, the boy saw, took wine and strange bread in very tiny portions and seemed overawed by the occasion. A small bell was rung at particular points in the service, and, eventually, the boy became an altar boy, and he rang the bell, hearing it echoing among all present, signalling the holiest of moments.

It was all so good, so obvious, and so compelling that the growing boy doubted not at all, despite there being, as he knew, some people who poured scorn on church-going and even doubted bits of the creed. It all had to be true, though sometimes the truth was difficult to grasp; only the Lay Reader and the Rector understood it fully.

His role in the little church strengthened; he was chosen to read lessons from the Bible during services and, eventually, to lead the whole congregation in prayer.

One Sunday he came out of Holy Communion full of the joy of the celebration and seeing the glory of God in all creation: the trees on the village green, the rustling leaves, and the blue, blue sky.

He tried very hard to follow the moral precepts that came with the whole story: honesty, faithfulness, and purity of mind.

In his teenage years, he started to feel the first twinges of guilt at moral failure, but nevertheless, alongside this, the main truth of the Christian story remained rock solid in his mind.

But why was the obvious truth of all his clear beliefs not more manifestly evidenced?

He asked God to show him such evidence through, perhaps, a miracle. He pledged that if such came, he would apply to be a priest. For a teenage birthday present, he asked his parents for his own prayer book.

But the miracle still did not come, so he came to live with a faith that was beset with doubt.

At university, he questioned everything, wanting to believe but wanting more intellectual reassurance. The Christian Union did not attract him - too much emotional baggage. He wanted intellectual clarity.

He did not find it.

All the classical "proofs" of God's existence fell before the onslaught of analytic philosophy.

He became an atheist and accepted that all that was left of religion, and all Christianity, was an ethical residue. This did, as he saw, seem reasonable, generous, and life-affirming, i.e., "love thy neighbour" - the Perennial Philosophy.

He felt nostalgic about the rites, ceremonies, music, and poetry of the Church of England. He particularly revered the old Rector who had led him into a better appreciation of Christian kindness and love. But this was a case of "the singer, not the song" through and through.

When the Rector, in retirement, paid a fleeting visit to his old parish and encountered the young university student on the village green, he asked the newly fledged atheist to consider the priesthood seriously. "The Church needs men," he said. He didn't know of his hoped for protégée's change of mind. The young man could say nothing except express his deep regard and admiration for his old guide and mentor.

Life itself, however, went on. The new graduate became a schoolteacher, married a fellow teacher, and embarked on a fully adult life without qualms.

Friends occasionally wondered why he had not gone into the church, and he always answered that he was far too sinful and that, in any case, he could not accept many of the literal beliefs apparently proffered by the clergy.

He still retained his aspiration to keep to the Perennial Philosophy. He thought, and perhaps hoped, that there might be some truth, but of a different, non-literal kind in the propositions of Christianity and, indeed, in the propositions of Islam, Buddhism, Hinduism, and other faiths. These great historic movements can be seen, he thought, as signs of a universal human need for an over-arching and overwhelming framework for understanding life.

He had read "Honest to God" by the Bishop of Woolwich, and thus knew that there were other ways than literalist, credal faithfulness to arrive at a more complete picture of the nature of human existence. Analytic philosophy and physics were not by themselves the only alternatives.

When he and his wife saw their little children starting to learn from the world about them, they looked for a non-credal way of entering something from which their children might come to be open to a wider view of things.

They started attending Quaker meetings with their children.

They were both almost immediately stunned by the power and depth of perception that comes with Quaker's silent worship. They both seemed to be entering into a deep awareness of aspects of life they were not previously very familiar with.

They stayed for the long term.

They became members and enthusiastic participants in Quaker activities. Their lives became punctuated by regular Quaker study groups, other Quaker activities, and regular silent worship.

The man himself began to reflect that in the deep silence of his worship, he could find, with others, a joyous awareness of the nature of all things that went wordlessly beyond the everyday, the material, the prosaic, and which seemed to embrace all people, all creatures, all the stuff of things, all time, and all space. Some, he knew, find this in various forms of meditation. The Quakers called it "spirituality," and he could go along with that.

It was a form of consciousness that he had only before found in listening to music or poetry or when overwhelmed by the beauty of the landscape, or trees, or the natural world, or the sky at night.

But there were no words to describe this awareness fully. He still remembered his joy as a youngster, after Holy Communion at his old village church, and saw that it was the same. But here it was with no creed, no obvious ceremony, no priest; it was an experience coming to him through his mere humanity. It gave him the strong experience of an all-embracing love for and from all things. It was a spur to "love thy neighbour," as well as, perhaps, a glimpse of eternity.

He had, as he thought, come home to a newfound spirituality, and this time, free of the clutter of creed and hierarchy. It was, perhaps, spiritual humanism, relying only on his own experience but taking him beyond himself into the universal - into "the silence of eternity, interpreted by love."

He began to think hard about how his acknowledgement of the spirituality of humankind could be reconciled with or expressed through the literal, credal, literally incredible tales behind the various faith traditions.

He tried to put down in words how these great traditions could still appeal to modern people born in the 20th and 21st centuries, with their widespread dismissal of the old religious stories and their more highly developed understanding of life in the material world.

The legends and stories of the religions and their most fundamental and central notions had to be interpreted in new ways to find anchorage in 21st century minds.

Here, he thought, is a job to be done, or at the very least attempted.

So here goes.

Part One:

The Allegory of God

Introduction

The American Quaker, Mulford Sibley, speaks in his article *Quaker Mysticism* of three stages of the development of a human's consciousness[1].

As very young infants, human beings universally make, he says, no distinction between themselves and the world outside themselves. All is one.

As we humans grow, we increasingly divide the outside world from ourselves. We come to see objects objectively, separating self from the other and clearly identifying ourselves as separate from the world as we grow into childhood, youth and adulthood. Science uses this universal paradigm in its objective search for a model of physical structure for the world, in its experimentation, measurement and observation.

Mystics, says Sibley, go further than this adult stage into a form of universal consciousness that sees beyond the objective world to perceive a transcendent reality that is more fundamental to our existence.

Here, in the first part of this book, we examine these latter two ways of perceiving the world: the objective and the mystical. We look at the uncertainties and the convictions involved in both and the limitations that seem to be part of being human.

From where does conviction arise? Where does uncertainty end if it does?

The conviction of scientists that the universe is governed by regularities or laws that are accessible to us is matched by the uncertainties around our capacity to find or understand all such regularities if they are there.

The conviction of mystics that there is a reality that transcends the immediate physical world is matched by widespread disbelief in the expressions of such conviction in words.

Language might be the key, for if we cannot describe what we think we see, how can we make sense of it?

Thus, we examine spirituality and the language of religion, and we examine science and its language.

Spirituality is, I think, a very individual response to existence. But it is often expressed through the language of *religion*, where religion is seen as an essentially communal response to existential questions. We will begin with God and the language of religion and only then move on to consider consciousness, experience and spirituality.

Then, we will look at science and its attempts at a complete explanation of our universe.

We will proceed to a general view, which may be thought to give validity to both while showing the limitations of every attempt we make at expressing our understanding of ourselves and our world.

The Allegory of God

What is happening here?

The room was silent. This profound silence was shaped by the quiet breathing of twenty people seated in a double oval. In the centre was a table bearing flowers, a Bible and *Quaker Faith and Practice*. This last is the book of discipline of the Religious Society of Friends and contains pieces of advice and queries for the consideration of members.

'Take heed, dear Friends, to the promptings of love and truth in your hearts. Trust them as the leadings of God... '[2]

A man stood up and spoke briefly, quoting the advice above and continuing the theme of truth in his own words.

He sat down.

Some heads bowed. Some eyes were closed. One woman stared straight ahead. Another slept.

In the half-hour since the meeting began, and in the half-hour yet to come, little had or would be spoken. Silence would envelop all present. Yet almost all would feel uplifted, at peace, even at peace with God, certainly renewed in personal strength for the struggles of the coming week.

This is a description of a typical Quaker Meeting for Worship in Britain at the present time. Sometimes, entire meetings pass in silence. More often, three, four or more people feel compelled to speak, briefly, to the meeting on what is in their heads and hearts.

But what is going on? Different people could give very different accounts if they were witnesses.

To a conventional Quaker, the meeting is waiting upon God, waiting in silence on the Spirit. Some Quakers would say that speakers wait to be led by God into what they say; the communal silence led by such ministry, when it occurs, is the 'Holy Communion' of the Society of Friends, a way, for some, of touching the hem of the garment of Jesus, of glimpsing that which is called 'the peace of God which passeth all understanding'[3], of seeing the world transfigured into a totally spiritual space.

A secular psychologist, maybe another Quaker, would use other languages entirely, speaking of calm and quietness certainly, but emphasising, perhaps, the separate individuals having a bit of space in which to let their minds and feelings settle in the loving company of like-minded friends. People may well feel better, calmer and stronger after an hour of this, but a more or less complete description can be given in these terms alone.

Other people would give yet other descriptions. Which is right? Which is valid?

There is no fundamental reason why several different descriptions may not all be valid. Given for different purposes and using different language, they appear to contradict one another but do not.

Let us take another example, a Vermeer painting. A description may be given in terms of light, colour, shape and so on, and their effect on those who see it, or in terms of the molecular structure of the paint which forms the surface of the work. Both may claim to be a full description in their terms, and both are valid. One does not directly contradict the other, though the exponent of one may deny the validity of the other.

The molecular scientist may say that talk of the light and the colour, and their distinctive effect on the viewer, is so much hooey, not something he can make sense of. The art critic who speaks of light and colour may say that talking about molecular structure is not in any way a discourse about the painting as a painting. Each can, indeed, seek to introduce the other to the language that he uses himself and the experience it signifies, but unless the other comes to accept the language, no progress will be made in mutual understanding.

The language in which we speak carries with it a structure and a set of assumptions that give discourse meaning, and there are, of course, differing languages in differing areas of discourse. Any explanation of an event, such as a Quaker meeting or a Vermeer painting, may be proposed from within one area of discourse, while proponents of another area can claim that explanation to be nothing.

Language is the key, and this is what we must now take further.

Language, Science and Religion

Humankind can be characterised in a number of ways, but one certainly valid characterisation is that we are language-using beings.

Language is a system of symbols standing in some relation to ideas and experience, and these symbols, appropriately structured, allow communication and thought. The idea that they allow communication is commonplace, though, of course, they are just one of a number of communication channels. One can communicate through the look on one's face or one's behaviour; interestingly, some aspects of these are often referred to as 'body language.' But when I am using the term 'language' here I am referring to the use of words, usually strung into sentences, expressed through speech or written signs.

It may be thought surprising, however, that we say language allows thought. Let us explore this.

The fundamental notion is that, in order to think, one has to have a language to think in. By thought or the thinking process, we mean the more or less rational processes involving notions of logic and argument and possibly drawing on experience. We do not, by thought, mean *any* mental state or process. It is perfectly possible, it would seem, to experience a mental process in which, say, fear develops without recourse to or access to any language. For example, a very young child, without language, can certainly exhibit what we call 'distress' and we would normally attribute real distress to the child as a person. So, perhaps, some processes which may be thought of as mental can take place without language.

What is being asserted here is that we have concepts, which are ideas or mental pictures of a group or class of objects. Rational thought is defined as the processing and manipulation of concepts according to rules: this cannot take place without language, without words signifying ideas standing in some relation to experience. You have to have something to process or manipulate.

A word and its concept are closely connected. A word is a piece of public property used, amongst other things, for communication amongst people. A word acquires its meaning through public use, and thus its meaning, or the concept it signifies, however vague, is a product of public activity, though it may originate in one person's head. Of course, language is not static but continually changing, with words changing their meaning, new words appearing, and new concepts being expressed and developed through new words and new uses of old words.

The thing to keep in mind is that rational thought and the concepts involved relate directly to language and its words. Language brings the possibility of rational thought. It is the manipulative framework within which rational thought occurs. So, when it is said that we are beings characterised by language use, we are also saying that we are characterised by the possibility of rational thought, i.e., we are rational beings.

It follows from these arguments that whenever we want to apply thought to an area of experience, we must have, or we must develop, a language to think our thoughts in. We have to develop concepts and, thus, words that we can use to refer to bits of the experience and then apply rules, particularly rules of logic, to the words and language we have developed so as to take our thoughts further.

Sometimes, we develop *explanatory* concepts and thus explanatory words, where we need to refer not to a piece of direct experience but to the result of thought about direct experience. This might be a situation where we need to explain some experience, and logic leads us to posit some notion that helps the explanation. An example of this would be the concept of an 'electron.' No one has ever seen an electron, though many have felt the force of an electric current. The concept of 'electron' is the product of rational scientific thought seeking to explain in great detail aspects of our experience of electricity. Scientists would assert that there exist electrons corresponding to the concept.

So language and thought develop together, new words and new concepts come into existence, and scientific explanation makes progress. The theories advanced today may be overthrown tomorrow by more comprehensive explanations, and new words and concepts may render the old redundant, but at least progress in the field of science is made by rational thought.

It is our thesis here that in the field of religion or spirituality, this is not so; for the language of religion and spirituality is utterly different from that of science, and the role of rationality is thus entirely other.

Let us now look at the language of spirituality and religion. That is our next port of call.

Religious Language and Experience

When we speak of religious language, we are thinking of terms like salvation, redeemer, soul, spirit, god, enlightenment, evil and eternity, with terms like insight, ecstasy, unity and the ground of our being often associated with the more individual and wider notion of spirituality.

In line with our previous treatment of language we should ask where this language and usage springs from. What sort of experience gives rise to religious language? We are, of course, asking about religious or spiritual experience, and here we are in an area which has its peculiarities. Religious or spiritual experience is not only difficult to define. It is an area of experience strongly affirmed by some and equally strongly dismissed by others. Some say that there is no such thing, or at least what masquerades as religious experience, can be adequately described in entirely non-religious terms; these people reject the validity of religious language altogether.

Of course, religious language is not uniform at all, even among learned religious practitioners. An Anglican monk may lay great stress on the concept of The Trinity, whereas a Jewish or Islamic cleric would see, at the very least, no need for the notion. The Tibetan Buddhist concept of reincarnation finds no place in the thought or language of Muslims, Christians or Jews. So languages vary across the spectrum of religions, and what separates us is culture and the different ways in which different cultures shape minds, language and thus ideas.

However, a moment's reflection tells us that we are all human beings sharing the same evolutionary history, with brains and senses developed in common. We can make progress by looking at what is, remarkably, similar between the experiences spoken of across world religions through the accounts of those whom I regard as the central groups in all religions, the mystics. Christian, Jewish, Islamic, Hindu, Taoist and Buddhist mystics have a remarkable amount to say, which is common to them all.

What may be called the primal experience of the world is in common, and it is through this primal experience that, it might be said, religious perception develops. Our experience of feeling a part of the large unity of the universe we see is in common with mystics of all religions. Prayerful meditation, using various forms, is common to Muslim Sufis and Christian monks, to Jewish rabbis and Buddhist lamas. Hindu holy men wandering through India may feel the same force of unity with all things as affects a Sikh or a Catholic priest.

It is suggested that it is through the various forms of meditative practice that fundamental religious or spiritual perceptions arise across the world. Commonly, it is said, there is felt a sense of peace and a sense of all-embracing love for one's fellow creatures, along with a need to share these feelings with others. Mystics of all religions speak of losing one's sense of self and of separation from others in an overwhelming perception that all of the universe is one interconnected, interpenetrating whole to which we all belong and into which our personality dissolves in love and peace.

Along with all this, mystics say a sense of time being of no importance and a sense that change, decay, and death are of no consequence arises because the moment in which the sense of self disappears in some way embraces all space and all time as well. Feelings of unutterable compassion for the suffering in the world and of a need to act in some way in relation to that suffering are common. It may be argued to all cultures across the world and to all types of mystical experience.

These common experiences of the nature of existence, one's relation to all things, and the emotions of, for example, love and compassion for all one's fellow beings appear to define the mystic's religious experience. The Alister Hardy archive of religious experience contains multiple examples of this across a wide population (as well as a varied and wider range of more complex, culturally determined experiences).[4]

What we are speaking of here is, arguably, the common source of religious culture across the world. It leads to the creation of whole religious systems and cultures with their own sets of ideas and their own languages. The same range of perceptions about existence via prayerful meditation leads, it is being argued, to Buddhist notions of dharma, enlightenment and Buddhahood; to Muslim notions of a unitary compassionate personal God; to Hindu notions of gods and goddesses to be respected and worshipped; and to Christian notions of salvation, redemption and sin. In each case, the ideas are formulated and expressed through a religious language characteristic of the religion. What is the relationship between what we have called the primal religious experience and the language and conceptual structure of the various religions that seem to have resulted? That is our next question.

The Universal Use of Allegory

When Christians speak of the birth of the Saviour to a virgin, when they speak of the Son of God coming to Earth as a baby to save sinners, they tell a powerful tale that resonates within the human psyche. The story tells us that God has revealed Himself through a babe in arms, and the only possible reaction to a baby is wonder and love. The story tells us that God, through a child, has great power but that it is up to us to accept that power in our lives. It tells us, above all, that God is a personal God, that the world is a personal creation and that God loves us. It tells us, in the end, that if we return God's love, we are ultimately forgiven and achieve salvation; loneliness, despair and death have been defeated. But all these feelings and reassurances are what come to men and women in prayerful meditation through the primal religious experience itself that we attempted to describe earlier. The sense of belonging, of love and peace, of wonder and power, of acceptance and eternity comes from the primal experience but is here expressed through Christian concepts, stories and beliefs. The Christian religion has developed a language in which to tell the primal story. The concepts, beliefs and structure which that language expresses constitute Christian theology. The almost inexpressible and ineffable primal perception has been mediated to us in terms we can take in, think about and develop.

The key notion here is that in order to communicate the primal experience to others and in order to think about it ourselves, we have to invent concepts, figures, stories and beliefs that allow us, at least partly, to hold the ineffable in words.

Of course, the particular circumstances of the beginnings of Christianity, with the historical Jesus of Nazareth and his tremendous vision, shaped the way the language and, thus, the belief system developed. Presumptions were made that derived from Judaism and started the whole thing off. But, once started, it developed into the complex tapestry of Christian belief and language, which itself now helps lead people towards the ineffable primal vision. Clearly, if it had not done this, it would not have lasted, for in each generation, people need to reach that vision in order to renew their faith.

The story of the birth of Christ, therefore, can be seen as an *allegory* about the nature of human existence and its relation to the universe, an allegory being defined here as a story used to communicate complex, fundamental and difficult ideas. This allegory attempts to express the ineffable. It attempts to express that primal religious experience, much of which is common to all societies, of a transcendent and yet immanent truth and reality beyond ordinary sense.

Other men and women, other cultures and other historical contexts lead to other allegories expressing related perceptions of the same experiences, each powerful and each leading people into what we might call the light. Thus, Islam, Buddhism, Hinduism, Sikhism and Judaism each have their own power to do this. Mahatma Gandhi said at one point, 'I am a Hindu and also a Christian, a Muslim, a Buddhist and a Jew.'[5] Perhaps we can come, through this discussion, to glimpse part of what he meant.

We should not come to assert that all these different traditions are, after all, paths to *my* truth, whatever that is. They are not all just other paths to Christian truth or to Islamic truth. They are all ways to come to understand possible paths towards the light, wherever that is.

So, when we said earlier that religious language is utterly different from that of science, we meant that religious language deals with allegories. These allegories illuminate the nature of existence, but they do not refer *directly* to that nature, for what is being spoken of is ineffable. Scientific language purports to deal literally with what exists; religious language deals allegorically with the nature of that existence.

How far can we take this account of religious language? Where does allegory end and literalism begin? Our proposal is that all conventional religious language is allegorical and that there is no room for literalism. What effect, if any, this has on the religious view of existence is part of what we will deal with in this work. But first, let us extend the notion of allegory by looking at examples from within major religious traditions.

Different Stories, the Same Insight

Within major forms of Buddhism, the notion of reincarnation is important. The individual on their journey toward enlightenment passes through many lives. The life you are leading now, with all its disappointments and failures, does not disbar you from nirvana, for it is only a small part of a much larger journey. That journey will have its ups and downs. It may last, in time, through millennia, but it is always ongoing, with an unimaginably perfect destination.

We say 'unimaginable,' but then, of course, we try to imagine it and describe it, to refer to it in words and to discuss its nature.

The point is that the notion of this journey allows people to move towards a genuine religious experience. It resonates with that experience and confirms it in notions that the mind can grasp and deal with. Buddhism provides an allegorical language which permits religious thought and leads people towards religious experience and a religious view of the world. If it had not done so down the ages, Buddhism, as a valid religion, would have disappeared.

The view of Allah as the only God, just, merciful and compassionate, also permits religious thought and, in exactly the same way, leads people towards religious experience and a religious life. When a Muslim speaks gently of the love of God and the need to care for all people with a regard for universal justice and compassion, he is expressing his understanding of a primal religious experience and its consequences, mediated to him by Islamic culture, belief and language.

All notions of heaven or paradise, be they Islamic or Christian in all their various forms, point to the relative unimportance of death and the relevance of a life guided by some sort of moral view. Resurrection, like reincarnation, underlines these perceptions. The story of the resurrection of Christ points dramatically to victory over death and, thus, over the restraints of time-governed life.

The notion of an allegory can, it is argued, be extended to all religions. To the extent that they illuminate the nature of human existence and resonate with the human psyche, religious beliefs consist of useful allegories, allowing thought and discourse and leading succeeding generations into a valid religious perception of the world. However, there are problems, of course. The very particular cultural origins of different religions lead to differing allegorical scripts. The operation of rational thought in the various schools of theology, operating on the particularities of differing allegories, produces structures of further ideas of great complexity and elegance. But, because we are applying rational thought to what is in essence ineffable, through its various allegorical concepts, we get contradictions and muddles, not only between differing religions but, of course, also within individual religious traditions. Theology often leads to contradiction and chaos, principally *because* religious perception is beyond thought, and religious language is metaphorical, not literal.

So Tibetan Buddhists differ from Zen Buddhists as well as differing from Hindus and Christians. Protestant Christians, of various sorts, differ from Roman Catholics, as well as differing from Judaists and Muslims.

These differences become great, cause wars and generate great suffering. But the mystics in all traditions can bring things together again by appealing to primal religious experience. This primal religious experience, beyond words and language, is the very perception, often framed by emotion, of peace, unity, love, timelessness and dissolution of self, which constitutes a religious perception of the world.

Theology, in the sense of a rational explication or a development of religious ideas, illuminates when its conclusions are clearly congruent with a primal religious experience. At its best it helps people into a deeper appreciation of the experience which hits them in the face. But it is the experience which has the greater authority, and theology that does not chime with experience is of little help and can, in fact, be damaging.

We say that experience has the greater authority, for it is that experience which, we may believe, gives hints of a transcendent spiritual reality, immanent in all existence, which is beyond words, but which many men and women of all cultures have proclaimed to their fellows.

The Allegory of Satan

Let us take as an example of an allegory the notion of Satan. Three centuries ago, most European Christians believed in the real existence of a person identified as Satan. The rebellious angel and source of all evil was seen as an objective being, continually interfering in the world and in each human being's personal affairs with the help of his minions. Principalities and powers were literally at work, attempting always to undermine the will of God by tempting humans to wrong-doing and thus condemning them to damnation.

It is certainly true today that most people, I think, including many believing Christians, do not take this view. Most believing European Christians will see Satan as a symbolic figure personifying evil and the power of evil in a useful and illuminating way, helping people to deal with their baser desires and impulses by seeing them as the works of an evil angel. But however useful and illuminating the allegory is, it is still seen as an allegory. There is, for most people, no belief in the objective existence of such a person.

The allegory draws attention to two things. The first is the importance of temptation to evil in all its forms. These are not just trivial peccadillos we are asked to countenance; they are assaults on our status as children of God. The second follows from the first. Temptation to evil is a spiritual matter. It is something that works to separate us from God, to damage us in our journey toward God, and to destroy us as inheritors of the Kingdom of Heaven.

So, the allegory of Satan, and, indeed, of all the devils and demons who work with him, dramatizes and highlights the nature of evil. It gives a framework within which people can discuss evil. *The Screwtape Letters* by C. S. Lewis[6] illustrates this better than almost anything else in the 20th Century, showing how the large and small temptations of life can lead to a slow decline away from the better life.

The fact that Satan is largely regarded as an allegorical figure now has not diminished the power of the idea of him. Evil is still real. It is still a spiritual matter of the first importance. It is still involved with human life and the conflicts within it. It is still of eternal significance in the order of things.

The fact that a piece of old religious realism has become an allegory in the minds of most Westerners does not diminish its force at all. Indeed, it has strengthened the idea in a world where scientific realism has cast doubt on literal interpretations. It has allowed a spiritual language about evil and its consequences to maintain its meaning and function.

Is there any limit to the notion of allegory? Is there any limit to our notion that allegory permits religious language, and thus useful religious thought, to flourish and be passed on through the generations? Where is the line between myth and reality? Or is the notion of such a line itself a mistake?

This is where we must go next, and this means that we must ask questions about our most fundamental religious notions and categories.

Is the Notion of Allegory All-embracing?

The most fundamental notions of religion (God, immortality, soul, enlightenment, salvation, incarnation, godliness, karma and so on) are, perhaps, all allegorical. They are features in various religious narratives written to communicate what mystics perceive and help others come towards that perception, i.e., that primal religious experience, beyond language, of what seems to be reality and truth.

That is a fairly bald statement, and it needs justification and illustration. We have already looked at some examples and outlined the general view that religious language is allegorical. But does this apply all the way through?

The notion of 'God' as an allegorical figure may be dismissed out of hand by some. Is it not, after all, yet another restatement of the thesis that 'God is dead' and to be rejected on the same grounds? Either religion is dead and to be dismissed, or religion is completely secularised and thus equally dead and to be dismissed?

It is the writer's view that these reasons for dismissal are mistaken. God is not dead. When we speak of God, we use language in the particular way outlined earlier to communicate aspects of the primal religious experience or mystical perception that cannot be otherwise communicated in words. To speak of the soul being saved by God's grace is to speak of the perception and sense of ineffable peace and forgiveness that is available to men and women coming to see the world and themselves in a particular way. It is coming to see that peace and forgiveness are somehow beyond time and are indestructible. Communication and thought become possible by using a language that enables mystical perception to be objectified into categories and beings.

So in my view God is not dead. He/She is as alive as ever in the thoughts and imaginations of humans. We may have created God, rather than the other way round, but, it seems, some of us need Him/Her and all that goes with this to express our perception of the transcendent.

This, it can be argued, applies to all religious concepts. The soul, immortality, karma, salvation, enlightenment, divine compassion, all feature in various religious allegories and all are means to communicating, expressing and thinking about a religious interpretation of existence.

Secularism and Spirituality

It is possible, of course, to live one's life in an entirely secular way without reference to any of the religious or spiritual realities or allegories I have described.

If religious traditions are reduced to their inherent ethical and compassionate content, then nothing beyond the normal moral concerns of everyday life is left. In this situation, it makes sense to stop speaking of religion completely. What is left is central to human life, of course. Important questions of morality, how one should live, relationships, responsibilities, and so on are very important but can be pursued in an entirely non-religious, secular context.

What is being said here is different and, in my view, far more real and significant. It is that religious language has an allegorical meaning, drawing attention to a spiritual perception or experience of life. This spirituality derives from a valid and transforming experience fundamentally different from other ways of seeing the world. It places one in one's proper place in the whole of existence. It is transforming because it transforms the way one lives. It transfigures the world. All comes to be seen as enduring significance beyond time and place, and this makes ultimate sense of the world.

Religion, therefore, is not to be secularised out of existence. It is one way of doing what all humans seek: to make sense of the world. The problems with this way only arise when we try to manipulate our expressions of it to build great theological structures out of the ineffable. Spirituality cannot be secularised away. Spiritual perception transforms the secular view. The perceptions of the mystics concerning the supremacy of love transform ethical discourse. Suppose love is the over-arching and central principle. In that case, ethics must be centred on it, and all particular ethical questions come to be, 'What does love demand?' the difficulties of the question, no doubt, remain. Still, now they are seen through a spiritual glass, and priorities may become clearer.

There is, therefore, an irreducible spirituality in a religious perception of the world. We should not be misled by the nature of religious language to reduce the religious view to nothing. When someone says 'God is Love'[8] and someone else replies that 'God is a hypothesis of which I have no need'[9] then both sincerely express a validly held perception of the world. The one does not contradict the other. The first expresses something of the nature of love and of existence; the second uses the term 'God' in a way inappropriate to its religious meaning. The second may demonstrate with science and logic the redundancy of the notion of God to a rational consideration of the world. Still, the first would argue that the notion of God expresses poetically something central to the spiritual view.

The mention of poetry is not accidental. The best expressions of religious allegory are to be found in the arts – poetry, literature, art, music, drama and architecture. The most vivid expressions of religion in the world are clearly to be seen in the temples, cathedrals, mosques, paintings, music and decorative art that exist in all cultures. See the languages of religion as our small and puny efforts to communicate in words what we do better through art; see that who we call 'God' is called by other names in other cultures; see beyond the literalism that has fogged the issue for most of human history; and then we may see our spirituality for what it really is.

We are, perhaps, at one: the Buddhist monk, the Sufi, the Sikh, the Quaker elder, the Hindu pandit, the Roman Catholic priest, men and women of all the major faiths. Do but see beyond the allegory, and we are at one.

The claims here are for a religious truth about a transcendent reality, immanent in all things, which is ultimately beyond words of any kind. But it is no less the truth. At his trial, Jesus was asked the central question, 'What is Truth?'. Perhaps in this discussion, we have inched our way toward understanding, in part, why that question is so important.

The conviction that ultimate reality is spiritual springs from wordless experience, and it is this conviction that the mystics of all religions have proclaimed to the world.

Consciousness, Experience and Spirituality

Subjective or Objective? The Puzzle of Consciousness

We have placed great emphasis on the conscious experience so far, which leads to the conviction that a transcendent reality exists. We should now look at the broad notion of conscious experience itself, i.e., how our conscious minds encounter what appear to be aspects of an external world and what seem to be aspects of our reaction to that encounter.

At the most basic level, we will first look at our experience of common or garden things like colour, shape, sound and smell, and reactions like anger, happiness, revulsion and horror. This will then lead to a discussion of spiritual experience.

The first group (colour, shape, etc.) is analysed by many philosophers as a fundamental sense experience, augmented by the conceptual frame we may impose on it. An example of the fundamental sense experience would be the taste of sugar, the look of a colour, or the taste of coffee, whereas conceptions around these (our notions of sugar like the temptations of it and its effect on food or drink; or our attitude to a certain colour or clothing of that colour) are in the conceptual frame we impose on our sense experience.

The first fundamental experiences, such as the look of a colour, are called by some philosophers *qualia*: the entirely subjective experiences of consciousness. It is impossible to analyse these experiences in objective terms since they are private experiences only accessible to the individual who has the experience. They are not available for study by objective science.

I know what my experience of yellowness is, but I have no access to the nature of your subjective experience of what we agree to call yellowness. It might be different. We can objectively agree that yellowness is related to electro-magnetic waves of a certain wavelength, but we can have no access to each other's private experience of the effects of such waves on our consciousness.

So, there are essentially private, subjective experiences of yellowness. We may agree on all the objects we have seen which have this consistent effect on us (we can agree on examples of yellowness), while still being completely unable to enter the private qualitative experience of yellowness in each other's consciousness.

So, qualia are private and subjective, but the common experiences involving them are sufficiently consistent for us to have a common language and a common word like 'yellow' to refer to our several separate private qualitative experiences of the qualia involved.

Our reactions to experience, in terms of emotion, can be similarly analysed into the entirely private, subjective and internal experiences (pleasant or unpleasant), and the conceptual frame within which we feel them.

An example might be fear. The private subjective experience of fear is unpleasant. But it is much more than simply an unpleasant feeling. Fear normally involves an object of fear and some beliefs about that object. We may be fearful about someone's possible actions, viewing them as cruel, unjust or merely unjustifiably painful for ourselves or others. We can talk with our fellows about the beliefs we have about these actions. What we have no access to, again, is the immediate, private, subjective quality of the feeling of fear in anyone other than our self. My fear may be an entirely different, though commonly unpleasant, experience from your fear.

In this way, I think it is possible to speak of *emotional qualia*, i.e. the private experience of the pleasant or unpleasant raw emotional response to stimuli.

In all this, both in sense experience and emotional experience, I am arguing that there are qualia which are essentially subjective, private experiences, inaccessible from one person to another, but forming the basic building blocks of our conscious experience both of the external world and of our internal emotional world of reaction to experience.

There are other aspects of conscious experience, such as logical thought, imagination and self-awareness. For now, I will only deal with sense experience and emotion, though we will return to self–awareness later.

For both sense experience and emotion, we are saying that there are internal, private, subjective experiences (the qualia), and an objective framework of inter-subjective reference where we can agree on an example of yellowness or fear without in any way knowing what each actually is in another person.

So, we have this gulf between the subjective and the objective view. Perhaps we can say that the first is the view from the inside (the qualia: sense experience or raw emotion), and the other is the view from the outside (the publicly discussable frameworks of reference for senses and emotions).

Brain and Mind

Among these publicly discussable frameworks is the highly important framework of ideas about the brain and, more precisely, about the neural events inside the brain that science tells us correspond to various conscious events (like seeing yellow or feeling fear).

The relationship between brain and mind, between neurology and experience, is central to the modern discussion of the objective/subjective division.

There is, as yet, no general agreement on the relationship between brain and mind, and there may never be. For our purposes, however, we have established that consciousness (the mind) experiences qualia, which are entirely private, while the objective frame of connected words and actions builds on this to allow language and social interaction.

When I fear someone's actions, I have:

a) A private experience of fear

b) Objective beliefs about the framework in the external world, which leads to my fear

c) Objective beliefs about my brain's corresponding neural activity, which medical technology can reveal.

It is being asserted that b) and c) are of the same kind in being beliefs about the objective world, whereas a) is private (and unavailable to objective investigation).

So far, we have encountered sense qualia and emotional qualia. Can this notion be extended into the spiritual sphere? That is where we must go next.

Spiritual Qualia?

Consciousness is clearly a mysterious experience. We all have it, but it defies definition. It may be that all conscious states have neural correlates in the objective biological world, but that does not negate the experience. We claim direct access to our own consciousness alone, with no access to anyone else's. Also, this access is *incorrigible*: we have experiences of qualia that are not open to doubt.

In an attempt to solve the consciousness mystery, some modern scientists have re-expressed consciousness as a collection of successive conscious mental states rather than a continuous unitary phenomenon and then asked whether there could possibly be unconscious mental states, as, for example, Freud proposed, with all the layers of theory that can be built on that notion.

The notion of unconscious mental states – the 'unconscious mind' – is a construct that does not seem relevant to our present concern, which has to do with actual conscious experience. It is the *experience* that we are trying to analyse, i.e., what human beings come face to face with. What is unconscious, if the notion is valid, is, by definition, outside of direct experience. Another piece of work may be waiting to be done on spirituality and the unconscious mind (vide the work of Carl Jung).

With all this in mind, perhaps, we are justified in ignoring the notion of the unconscious mind for our present purposes while acknowledging its place in some areas of thought.

So let us get back to consciousness, whether of sense qualia or emotional qualia. Each might be thought of as a different sort of qualia, thus a different conscious mental state. Can one go further and think about other sorts of qualia?

The sorts of emotions we have considered have always involved an object, e.g., one is fearful of someone or something and what he, she, or it might do. Some philosophers have characterised this as being *intentional*, which means simply directed towards an object. One fears a loose, wild tiger or is angry with another human.

But some emotional states appear object-free, for example, various moods such as anxiety, happiness or joy. These may sometimes be entirely general and without particular objects.

And these moods often seem of *existential* significance: one can be simply anxious about everything and all aspects of one's experience in such a way that all existence seems painful and thus, perhaps, pointless. At the opposite end of the emotional spectrum, one can feel a very generalised joy about simply existing or being so that the whole of one's experience needs no explanation or justification: it is simply a source of joy, or, indeed, it is joy itself.

We are in familiar territory here. This is one of the sorts of experiences that mystics talk about, a generalised and heightened mood or emotion of joy or happiness.

It is being argued here that these experiences are just as private, incorrigible and compelling as those of intentional emotions or sense qualia.

Now, of course, reports of the experiences which might be called 'spiritual' and which we have enumerated earlier are normally surrounded by cultural frameworks of reference related to the religious or spiritual background of the subject. But what we have found is that there are strong commonalities between the accounts given: joy and peace; unity with all things and all people; a feeling that time is gone; all space is embraced, and the self is dissolved; and a feeling of benevolence to all of existence. All these have been mentioned in our previous discussion of spiritual experience. When the cultural frameworks are stripped away these are left.

Thus, we are arguing that these commonalities can usefully be described as *spiritual qualia*. These are completely private experiences and incommunicable to others who have not had similar experiences, and they are as incorrigible as our private experiences of fear or the colour yellow.

The experience of peace and unity cannot be communicated to another who has not had the experience, any more than the experience of the colour yellow can be communicated to someone blind since birth.

The sense or feeling of unity with all that exists links with the experience of the dissolution of the self, which needs to be examined more closely. One major common characteristic of normal conscious experience is that of being *self-aware*. It is a powerful and all-embracing characteristic of one's normal consciousness in which the self is separate from the world around one. But, commonly, in the sphere of spiritual experience, it is the *dissolution of the self* that is remarked upon, an equally powerful and all-embracing experience: the self is dissolved into a conscious experience so that one's consciousness becomes the experience, becomes the universe as seen in all time and space. There is no division between consciousness and all that exists. This is a change in the form of consciousness and seems to characterise spiritual states of being; within this changed form of consciousness come feelings of love, benevolence and peace, all seen in a moment, in the now.

All this, it is argued, makes up spiritual qualia, a change in the *form* of consciousness, with the concomitant feelings and perceptions described above. And these spiritual qualia are, of course, private and incorrigible, as are all qualia.

Universal Spiritual Qualia?

Let us now examine the position of such spiritual qualia in our understanding of things.

It might be argued that these spiritual qualia are very different from other things we have called qualia because they are certainly not universal: they are, indeed, uncommon in most human experience and are even uncommon in any one individual's experience. But similar things can be said about other sorts of qualia. It is uncommon in any individual's experience to feel existential terror, but one would not, as a consequence, rule out such a feeling.

We are not going to argue that what we have called spiritual qualia are the same sorts of experience as the experience of yellow or fear. We would argue, though, that spiritual qualia are private and incorrigible, and their uncommon nature is no reason to dismiss them as invalid: they are a real and compelling phenomenon of private experience that can shape one's perception of existence.

So we have, perhaps, established the validity of spiritual qualia, i.e., there are conscious experiences which can lead to a spiritual interpretation of existence.

Two sets of questions now arise:

1) How widespread is the phenomenon of spiritual experience? 2) Spiritual or religious interpretations of life have commonly and historically led to notions of ethics and community values

How can our account fit in with such developed notions of ethics and the human community?

These are new sets of questions for us to look at, and first, we will take a look at how widespread such experiences are.

Systematic Evidence for Common Spiritual Experience

It is clearly the case that conscious spiritual experience is a frequently repeated phenomenon across human history, and we have already nominated the testimonies of saints, holy men, mystics, prophets and other writers as well-regarded examples of what we have called spiritual qualia.

But what of you and me? In the midst of our ordinary, everyday life, we may have experience which is *unremarked*, but which is nevertheless *remarkable*.

An attempt has been made to catalogue remarkable experiences in this sense. The Alastair Hardy research project into religious experience, which we mentioned earlier, has collated thousands of short accounts volunteered by respondents as descriptions of their own spiritual experiences.[10]

These accounts are very varied and include people from a particular religious background or none. They are normally expressed from within a cultural/religious context and use the language and imagery of that context. But, as with our previous examples from mystics, prophets and holy men, there is a widespread commonality of the spiritual qualia which we have been citing. Happiness, joy, calm, peace, benevolence, timelessness and selflessness crop up over and over again for both men and women.

More research is needed here, but it seems that many people, when asked, will reveal a spirituality in their lives which might not have been suspected.

Some of the reports, it must be said, are of negative experience: anxiety, fear, even dread and anger are there. One must ask about the significance of these feelings. Perhaps there is what some might call *spiritual terror*. This appalling sort of experience may be what some theologians have called *separation from God*. For the people concerned, these feelings are clearly of existential significance.

Perhaps we should start to speak of existential experience rather than spiritual experience, embracing both the positive and the negative. We will speak more of this later.

Ethics and Community Values

With positive experiences, we can be clear that they have significance for both ethics and for community.

The widespread mention of feelings of general benevolence can clearly lead to a benevolent code of ethics. If one's best perception of the world is framed in benevolence, then one's morality is going to be framed in terms of the Golden Rule, the Perennial Philosophy and 'love thy neighbour'. One can come to see the love of God, the compassion of Allah or the benevolence of Buddhahood as the way or ways to follow in one's conduct in the world.

Further, these spiritual qualia, these feelings of benevolence, of peace, of love for all people and of love for all living things, can lead to a sense that we are all together; we are not in competition but in brotherhood and sisterhood, in community.

So, the messages of women and men of faith in a morality based on love and common humanity can be seen as emerging from spiritual experience, as reported in the various scriptures: we have the beginnings of a society's over-arching moral and social framework.

The Negative Experience

The positive aspects of our spiritual qualia are thus clear. But we have also noted that some reported experience is existentially negative. Fear, terror, anguish and anger are mentioned, and these are, for many people, it seems, equally as determining of their spiritual perception of things.

These negative emotions are, again, commonly reported as objectless. Generalised benevolence and love felt for the whole world, without a particular object, is mirrored negatively by a generalised anguish or despair about the whole of existence without a particular object in view.

Perhaps here, we need to take a major step. Spirituality has both negative and positive aspects, so it has both bad and good results in the human psyche. In traditional terms, one can feel oneself to be separated from God, as we previously said, or to be united with God: both are spiritual experiences.

Perhaps in restricting the word 'spiritual' to the positive aspects of such existential experience, we have concentrated on what we may aspire to.

Perhaps the more general term to cover both good and bad experiences is simply 'existential' or maybe the phrase 'fully human'. Maybe we should say that to be fully human is to be open to both joy and despair in matters of existential consciousness. But we know that the happier conclusion is to see the world, the universe, as joy, and perhaps that is all the mystics, saints, and the founders of major religions have been trying to tell us all along.

In traditional language, there is both heaven and hell available to you. The advice of the saints is 'choose heaven'.

Good spiritual experience will lead you in that direction.

The Language and Reach of Science

Ordinary Language and Reality

We have outlined the way in which a spiritual view of the world may develop and mentioned how it can inform ethics, morality and a strong positive sense of community.

But for many of us who may not usually use spiritual language, the everyday world in which we live seems to be the way things actually are. This everyday world of sticks and stones, food and drink, paths to walk along, and other people – the ordinary objects of our normal five senses – seems to be the ultimate reality.

'I believe in what I can see and touch. There is nothing else, nothing other than this, to consider.' This is a common conviction. Let us examine it.

The table on which I am writing might be described as made of solid wood, with a flat, hard surface on which my writing pad rests. I hold a long, thin, hard ballpoint pen in my hand and press on the pad to make marks that I can see.

If I go outside, I walk on hard ground. I may kick a stone down the path. I feel the hardness of the solid stone, and I can feel the softness of the leaves on the bushes on my drive. 'Get used to it and deal with it! I am convinced that this is what ultimate reality is.'

Indeed, we have to deal with reality all the time and have always had to. As a species we developed organs and senses that allow us to deal with the physical world we live in. We survive and thrive by dealing with that world.

When we come to science, much of the ordinary world we have just described is included. For example, the concept of hardness is used in the science of geology to help us identify rocks and minerals. Equally, kicking a stone down a path can be expressed in terms of energy: we know that the energy we have in our foot is converted into the movement of the stone.

But science goes much further than this. 19th and 20th Century physics tells us that all matter is made of atoms, usually combined into molecules. Each atom consists of a nucleus with an electron or electrons orbiting around it with a great gap between the orbits and the nucleus. Each nucleus consists of protons and neutrons bound together by various forces, and further analysis reveals even more basic particles that constitute the real world.

According to this physics, the reality is that this solid rock is, in fact, more than 99.9% nothing! The notions of solidity or hardness are ideas we have imposed upon an external world that appears more fantastic and, indeed, more fantastically strange than we ever thought. Albert Einstein once said, in a wider context, something like 'Reality is merely an illusion, albeit a very persistent one'.[11]

So, the language of reality we developed to deal with everyday experience only partially corresponds to the reality that, on scientific grounds, we believe to exist.

Everyday language tells us that lead and gold are very different, and, incidentally, one cannot be changed into the other except by wizardry. Nuclear physics tells us that the two metals are made of the same stuff and, given the right conditions, one can indeed be changed into the other.

So let us now look in more detail at the language of science.

A Success Story

The story of science over recent centuries is one of developing an ever more successful understanding of the physical world despite the blind alleys that scientists have gone down from time to time.

Our present way of life could not have occurred without the success of science and its application to engineering and technology.

The manifest success of all this is before us every day. The ballpoint pen I am using at this moment depends on the forging and engineering of ever more sophisticated metal and plastic, to say nothing of the ink.

So, how does science work?

Scientific Method

Science seeks, by observation and experiment, to establish what regularities there are in our experience of the objective, physical world. Grouping such regularities together, scientists strive to construct theoretical models of the world, which can then be used to predict future events. The private world of consciousness is, we would argue, beyond this investigation.

For example, the observation that free-falling bodies accelerate toward the ground at the same rate may lead to confirming experiments and then lead to the construction of a model of how gravity works and the positing of rules or laws which the physical world appears to follow.

Those laws (e.g. Newton's Laws) can then be used to predict future events (e.g. how long a cannonball will take to drop from a fortress wall or when a solar eclipse will occur).

If a lot of predictions prove correct, then, to that extent, the law is supported by evidence. A prediction that proved to be mistaken, where the event is not as predicted, will cause further thought and possible re-modelling, or revision of the law, to account for this apparent aberration.

All this has been in aid of establishing patterns of cause and effect so that regularities can be systematised into an ever more complete model of the bit of the physical world being investigated.

What is being done, always, is building theoretical models of the world, so that our understanding of events in the physical world is developed.

What causes produce what effects? If questions like this can be answered through observation and experiment, then science advances.

Cause and Effect

The notion of cause and effect is, however, puzzling in itself.

Philosophers like David Hume, in the 18th Century, examined this and found that the connection between an effect and its posited cause is unanalysable, except as a consistent contiguity in time and space. In other words, the effect and its cause occur together regularly or consistently, and nothing more can be said.

This is neatly in line with what we have previously said, that science seeks to identify mere regularities in the physical world. This is precisely what investigating events (effects) and their causes comprises.

Causality, it seems, is nothing more than the regular linking of physical events. Our language may lead us to believe in some sort of organic (or necessary) connection, but the connection is only contingent, i.e., it occurs in our experience and is true by virtue of the way things are experienced.

Modern Science

In the grand scheme of modern science, vast and complex theoretical models have been built on the basis of universal causality. This is fine and has been, as was said earlier, hugely successful, with triumphs in engineering and technology, which have transformed the world in which we live.

There seem to be problems, however, with fundamental physics.

Famously the theories of Isaac Newton about gravity were found to be only approximately true. Further observation and, importantly, mathematical calculation showed that, though hugely useful in everyday life and engineering, the theories were inaccurate in certain situations.

With successive leaps of imagination, Albert Einstein developed his special and general theories of relativity, which accounted for these anomalies. Again, science then progressed to a better understanding of the world.

So far, so good. One set of theories and its derived models was displaced by an apparently better set of theories and models. Subsequent evidence of observation supported the new theories.

Relativity triumphed, particularly in respect to observations of the universe on a large scale. Here, we are speaking of stars and planets, galaxies and groups of galaxies, and the whole universe.

The general theory of relativity also led to developments in technology, which are now all around us every day.

The notion of space/time, the warping of space and the idea that time seems to travel faster or more slowly depending on the relative velocities of the observed and the observer have led, for example, to really accurate satnav navigation. Without relativity, satellite positioning of your car could be no more accurate than perhaps a quarter of a mile, whereas, as we know, our position can be pinpointed within a very few yards or less.

So science led to useful technology, which, in turn, gives us confidence in science.

Alongside the development of relativity, early in the 20th Century, large developments also occurred in the theoretical physics of the very small.

Looking at the world of sub-atomic particles led to what is normally called quantum theory, dealing with electrons, protons and neutrons, together with other fundamental particles such as quarks, muons and so on.

Developed by a number of people, including Einstein, and in a rather fragmented way, quantum theory suggests that the world of sub-atomic physics is not like the clockwork world of everyday life.

In everyday life, we deal with objects consisting of very large numbers of particles, where ordinary cause and effect, as commonly understood, seems to hold sway.

In the quantum world, qualities such as energy occur in specific set amounts, and change involves a *jump* from one quantified amount to another rather than the smooth continuous change posited by classical physics. In the quantum world, light can behave as a particle as well as a wave. In quantum theory, matter, which consists of sub-atomic particles, can sometimes behave as a wave. For example, the way electrons whizz round the nucleus of an atom cannot be explained by classical mechanics, but scientists developing quantum theory showed that electron behaviour could be accounted for by treating electrons as a species of a wave, producing uncertainty about normal classical measurements of position and speed. Indeed, Heisenberg's Uncertainty Principle states that the more precisely an electron's position is known, the less precisely its speed can be known, and vice versa. Whether this is a result of difficulties of observation or of an underlying uncertainty is still contested, but only by a few scientists.

If you are confused by all this, you are not alone. Even the great physicist Richard Feynman said, 'I think I can safely say that nobody understands quantum mechanics.'[12] And Niels Bohr, a pioneer of quantum theory, said, 'those who are not shocked when they first come across quantum theory cannot possibly have understood it.'[13]

But again, like relativity, the science of quantum mechanics has led to technology which is all around us every day, including lasers, fibre optics, DVDs, MRI scanners and more.

So we have two great sets of theories from the 20th Century, relativity and quantum theory, the first dealing well with the very large and the second dealing well with the very small.

Conflict

But the two separate theories have so far defied unification: they appear to involve incompatible descriptions of reality. Relativity adopts a classical theory of causality that causes produce specific contiguous effects, that events are determined, and that the universe is deterministic. Quantum mechanics, however, allows connections between events without reference to classical causality and also allows that outcomes of sub-atomic activity involve genuine uncertainty.

Recent experiments have shown two electrons affecting each other at a distance and instantaneously. The uncertainty principle itself seems to defy any deterministic theory based on classical causality.

Efforts by physicists to make progress in seeking a grand unifying theory, embracing and reconciling relativity and quantum theory, have so far failed. These efforts continue and may see some success in the future. Current efforts via what is called string theory (where fundamental particles are seen as one-dimensional *strings* subject to a variety of vibrations and existing perhaps in a multi-dimensional world) at present lack supporting empirical evidence.

So where do we go next?

The Problems and Limits of Human Scientific Enquiry

It may be that we need to look at the limitations of humans in our search for explanation and, indeed, to look at these in two related ways:

- Limitations of language

- Limitations of intellect

In respect of language, it is the case that the English language (and perhaps any human language) deals with relativity and quantum mechanics with great difficulty.

That time can travel faster or slower is contrary to the common experience that language is built on.

That the position of a particle is a matter of uncertainty, a matter of statistical analysis, a matter affected, possibly, by the act of observation: these things are also contrary to that same common experience.

But, of course, all human languages have developed to deal with our common everyday world of large solid, liquid or gaseous objects, with time proceeding steadily forward.

Our languages are, then, not ideally fitted to deal easily with either the relativistic universe or the uncertainty principle.

Perhaps the very structure of our languages prevents us from describing and analysing the phenomena we encounter at the very large and at the very small scale. Maybe we will need to invent a new language before we can better understand these phenomena. Or maybe the only way to describe these phenomena is to use the language of mathematics? For it is clear that all our worlds – the very large, the every day, and the very small – are structured mathematically.

There is also, of course, our second limitation. The intellectual ability even of our brightest scientists depends on their brains and how their brains have been nurtured during their short lives.

The human brain is an immensely complex organ. At a Royal Astronomical Society conference recently one speaker told me that, of all the objects in the known universe, the human brain is the one with the most complex structure. I found myself thinking that this is a misstatement. The most he can say is that the human brain is a more complex structure than anything else in the *model* of the universe that science suggests to us.

Our knowledge of the universe is based on theories in physics, and these theories suggest a model or models, which are the best we can do in describing the universe.

It is no surprise that our human brains seem to have discovered nothing more complex than they are themselves. Can they, indeed, possibly posit structures more complex than their own structure? There would not be enough information-holding capacity to hold the information about structures more complex than that of the information-holding capacity itself.

But, maybe one thinks computer systems, or artificial intelligence, can hold enough information, or problem-solving capacity, for us. However, stored information is not conscious knowledge, nor is problem-solving conscious understanding.

So, it may be that the universe is more complex than the human brain can possibly comprehend. If this is so, then perhaps the search for a general unifying theory is doomed to failure.

So, if we consider the way our human brains have developed, we reach a startling conclusion. We have evolved from chemical cocktails over millions of years, and we have considerable capacity to understand the world in which we exist.

But there is no necessity for the idea that we will evolve sufficiently powerful brains to completely understand our physical universe. It may never happen.

So, there may be limits of brain capacity, as well as limits of language, which will prevent us from attaining a thorough and complete understanding of our physical universe: we may never get there.

And this is beside the impossibility of objective investigation of private consciousness.

However, the scientists' fundamental conviction remains, amidst all this uncertainty, that physical laws govern the universe, and we can, in principle, discover them.

A Scientist's Spirituality

"I still have a sense of the Numinous"[14]

Jocelyn Bell Burnell, Astrophysicist, discoverer of Pulsars

"I am a deeply religious non-believer"[15]

Albert Einstein

There are scientists who, faced with the plasticity of space and time, the uncertainty principle, the continual interplay between mass and energy, dark mass, dark energy and all the difficulties of language and intellect, are nevertheless powerfully struck by the unity of things and come to see themselves and their own consciousness as a tiny bit of this unity. They approach what might be called a scientist's spirituality.

They can, indeed, come to be in that mode of consciousness and perception, which subsumes them into the flux of existent reality. This can be described as a spiritual view of existence in which the ultimate structure of reality is seen as implicitly and silently beyond the world of systematic and objective observation and belief. This is, perhaps, what Einstein called *cosmic religion*.[16]

Spirituality, it seems then, is universally available: through prayer or meditation, through the insight and vision of many scientists, through the everyday experiences in ordinary lives of, for example, the arts, the landscape and the night sky, or in community activities and relationships.

Within this spirituality there may arise religious conviction. There will almost certainly arise a commitment to truth and to the perennial philosophy of general benevolence. A better way of living will beckon.

Conclusion

Connections

So far, we have looked at religious and scientific approaches, with a brief mention of the everyday. But how do these different approaches inter-relate?

A religious interpretation, or the perception on which it is based, may, in some respects, be placed alongside an everyday 'common sense' perception of the world. It may supplement that perception in the sense that it informs and changes the way we see things in the natural, social or personal worlds in which we live. A thorough scientific perception of the world may, of course, have a similar type of effect on one's everyday view of things.

By *perception*, here is meant the underlying framework within which basic sense experience and basic emotional experience are categorised. It is these basic sense and emotional experiences that make up the raw material of our consciousness, and part of this is the primal religious experience at the heart of my account of things.

When a mystic perceives what she calls universal love, universal peace or an ocean of darkness, she and her fellow mystics may express the underlying primal experience through her created language, giving form to her sense of the nature of things and thus expressing her religious perception of existence.

When a scientist perceives previously unobserved regularities and relationships in the physical world, she and her fellow scientists then express this perception through the equally created language of science.

The difficulties in relating the languages of science and religion originate in the different language functions performed. The language of science is realist; that of religion expresses allegory. All religious language is in this category, but nevertheless, referring to primal experience, it suggests to us the reality of the transcendent and, thus, the validity of a religious interpretation of the world.

A thorough-going and exclusively scientific view of the world is a valid view, of course, but it cannot be successfully argued that a religious interpretation of the world is invalid by those whose experience has not included experiences giving rise to religious language.

In a similar way, those who have never been in love cannot deny the validity of the viewpoint of a lover and the language, apparently incomprehensible, he or she might use about the beloved. To the lover, the perfection of the loved one can be as important in life as electricity, perhaps more so. It defines the nature of living, it maps the future, it is more important, sometimes than life itself. It is not being argued that being religious is like being in love, but that, in terms of the nature and function of language, parallels exist.

So, immortality is an allegorical way of expressing the notion that death is of no consequence for spiritual reasons. Salvation expresses the notion of universally available spiritual peace, and so on. Both, like all religious language, point to an inexpressible transcendent reality and the entirely valid view of the world entailed by such a possible inference.

Of course, when theologians in all religions start applying systematic, rational thought to the allegorical notions that are created, they sometimes come to bizarre conclusions; theological disputes result in opposing and equally unjustified conclusions being matched against each other. Thus, churches split, wars took place, and people were burned and slaughtered.

But theological and religious discord, based on different cultural allegories or different interpretations of the same allegory, do not, in themselves, invalidate the primal spiritual experience or the basic religious view of the world. It is when we start to speak of it that we may get into a muddle. As Ludwig Wittgenstein famously wrote: *"Whereof one cannot speak, thereof one should be silent."*[17]

Summary

We have, so far, in this little book, looked at two large areas of language and understanding, spirituality and science.

In both cases, there are problems about the extent to which our efforts to understand our world are hampered by the language we use and, indeed, perhaps, problems about the extent to which we are misled by language. Uncertainty often prevails.

Our everyday language helps us to live our lives in the everyday world but may mislead us about that world's nature, as science tells us it is.

We should be chary of applying this everyday language to religion and spirituality and equally chary about applying it to the complex world of modern physics.

We need different languages in religion and in physics, perhaps a language of allegory through the arts for the first and perhaps a mathematical language for the second.

Let us be clear about these differences, and then we may make progress in understanding our existence and, perhaps, understanding ourselves.

But, in the end, it may be that both the arts and the mathematics we are capable of may be insufficient for the purpose. It may be that the truths of existence and of science are beyond any language we can invent. It may be that the stories we tell ourselves in all these areas simply help us to make limited sense of the world, as does ordinary language in our ordinary world.

It is only through wordless spirituality, perhaps, that we can come to real insight, as have the mystics of all ages.

We are humble beings. The nature of our existence remains something of a mystery. In our individual brief lives, all we can do is strive together to address the existential puzzles with which we are presented.

Let us joyously accept the convictions that come through the wordless spirituality of all things.

The spiritual wonder of the world, of our lives, remains. Let us acknowledge and accept that wonder.

Interlude

The Problem of Graven Images

It has always struck me as rather odd, at least, that many Christian communities, having been told in the Bible not to "take unto thee any graven images," have filled their churches with such things.

They are often stunningly beautiful portrayals of saints of various kinds. I remember a striking painting of St Catherine. This is, of course, a painted image rather than a graven image, but the problem as I see it applies to both.

In stone, I think of the amazing figure of the Pieta: St Mary the Virgin, cradling the dead Christ, in St Peter's Basilica in Rome. Whether they be paintings or sculptures, the use of images is widespread.

Contrast this with the almost total absence of images in mosques: an absolute refusal to even try to portray God. In the vast majority of Mosques, no images of people at all, whether of highly regarded people or even of Mohammed himself.

Images of the Christian God are, however, famous: the picture of God the Son lying dead in his mother's arms, or the creator touching the finger of Adam as he instils life into Man in the Sistine Chapel, and, also there, the picture of the Last Judgment with the hand of Christ in majesty passing judgment on sinful humankind.

But you might object, indeed, that a lot of what you have mentioned are paintings, not actual graven images.

Actually, solid, graven or similar images are ubiquitous in apostolic churches across the world.

Go into any such church, and you will find a wooden or metal image of God the Son hanging on a cross on the altar.

These solid images of God the Son are actually the very centre of worship.

Indeed, go into any such church when there is a service in progress and you will find large or small crowds of people bowing down or kneeling before these graven images.

I remember a hymn that berated the "heathen" for bowing down "to wood and stone" in their ignorance, and yet it happens every Sunday across the world in Apostolic churches.

Why are such images absent from Mosques and most non-apostolic churches but present in many mainstream churches?

Of course, they are also absent from Synagogues, and here, perhaps, is the clue.

According to the originating documents of Abrahamic religions, God is impossible to model or picture.

"I am that I am."

If you make images or models of the God-Head, you are, it is said, limiting God. In all such faiths, God is thought of as unlimited, universal, ever-present, and everywhere present. If you have imagined God in a particular form and made an image of Him/Her in that form, you have clearly made a grave mistake. You have limited God.

It will be said in reply that these images are not worshipped --- they are merely symbolic of that which is worshipped. The image of God the Son on the cross 'stands for' the crucified Lord, the sacrificed Son, and so the image is not itself being worshipped.

There is a problem with this.

I remember one of my teachers at school (a very learned and devout Anglican) telling us that heaven is unimaginable. "We cannot possibly know what heaven is like" he said, and we thus cannot know what God, or the risen Christ, is like, he could have added.

But when we use "symbolic" images of these Beings we create, I think, "graven images" in our minds. This is the problem.

The image of Christ on the cross gives us the mental image that we carry around with us. And this mental image, graven in our minds, is as powerful as, or more powerful than, I think, than any stone or metal graven image.

But why do the Abrahamic religions object to graven images in the first place?

The answer has already been given.

Any image of God created by humans is limited in its qualities, and any such image, if accepted, is likely to limit our idea of God. On the contrary, "I am that I am "suggests that God is nameless, unlimited in power and presence, embracing all existence.

The images, graven or painted, simply reinforce our invented ideas of Divine Beings, taking us away from the central notion of general spirituality, universally available and powerful in its generality, to which we can, individually, come very close.

Part Two:
Mind, Brain, and Spirit

Introduction

In Part One of this work, we established that a spiritual view of the world and of ourselves is a valid view. We came to the view that "the wordless spirituality of all things" can lead us to a universalist religious conviction. We noted the failure of science to account for awareness or consciousness. Consciousness we saw as central to our account, it being the means of spiritual perception through the widespread human experience of a change in the form of consciousness through meditation, worship, prayer, or, we suggested, various forms of art.

We are now going to explore a possible account of consciousness, linking brain and mind, proposed from within the scientific community, which may help us with our picture of things. Or it may not. We will find that, if accepted, this account might be seen as leading to startling conclusions about the nature of the universe and everything in it. In old-fashioned language, the conclusion might be that God is everywhere, in all creatures and all things. Or it might not.

We will thoroughly explore this proposal to see any possible ramifications for our view of spirituality. We will undertake this exercise with great care, for it will be easy to stumble into misapprehension.

So, let us begin.

Brain and Mind

In Part One, again, we indeed, looked briefly at the question of connections between brain and mind. We said that there is little if any, agreement among scientists and philosophers on this.

Surgeons, in their work, have never found anything they could call a 'mind' inside the skull, and philosophers, in their discussions of 'mind', have often disagreed about whether the word 'mind' stands for anything at all.

Yet, each of us is convinced that we have a mind. We experience "To have a mind" "He has a mind of his own." "Will you make up your mind?" "Don't mind me".

We THINK, either carefully or, often, carelessly. We make choices and decisions; we have feelings, and we love, and we experience being CONSCIOUS of doing all this.

None of this is observed by the surgeon.

In fact, we ourselves cannot observe any of this in each other, either. All we can actually OBSERVE is each other's behaviour: the actions involved, the facial expressions, the speech.

So, some philosophers have taken the view that the 'mind' is simply an idea that has developed to designate just these forms of human behaviour. It is, they say, a pure behaviourist idea. We could say (like a behaviourist) that someone or something "has a mind" if we see intelligent behaviour, i.e., see evidence in behaviour (including speech), that someone/something is making what we see as choices, or taking attitudes, or feeling emotions, or loving. There is nothing more to it than that, however complex it is. They say the word 'mind' refers to nothing inside us. It is just a short-hand descriptive word for what we see in external behaviour.

Further, some other philosophers have suggested that even if there IS a private individual 'inside' each of us, we can say nothing at all of this; only the behaviourist account is valid. This may be a very important point, as we will see later.

But we know, as we have just said, that we are conscious of our own mental processes, and perhaps, it is CONSCIOUSNESS, which is the key idea here, as we have previously argued.

Mind and Spirit

Some theologians (in contrast to behaviourists) speak of the 'spirit' or conscious mind of each of us and in each of us, and they are not surprised at all that the surgeon finds no mind in the skull.

I have said 'spirit' as an alternative to 'mind' here; 'spirit' is taken by many to be the animating principle that gives 'life' to mere physical flesh. There is ambiguity and some vagueness here, but I take 'spirit' to refer to that in and of each of us which is aware of the spirituality and spiritual experience we have discussed in Part One.

Two Worlds?

There are two worlds, these theologians say: that of the flesh (for the surgeon to investigate) and that of the 'spirit' (or perhaps 'mind'), which is, they say, their own realm of expertise and discussion. I take 'spirit' and 'mind' here to be two expressions of the same idea of a possible non-physical world.

Lots of problems arise out of positing two worlds, however.

If there are two worlds, i.e., the mental or spiritual world and the physical world of the brain, how do these two worlds interact? How does, for example, my non-physical mind make a conscious decision to make my legs start to run when I try to catch a bus (i.e. to make my brain send physical messages to my leg muscles)? In other words, how does a conscious mental/spiritual event bring about a physical event?

Mind/Brain causality is a real problem in a' two world' duality.

One World?

So maybe there are not two worlds, but just one.

Common experience supports this view. We have all, I guess, seen examples in life where, in illness, the development of a positive attitude has brought about a physical improvement in a patient, i.e., where the mental/spiritual has affected the physical.

And, of course, it goes back to our first example: how my mind's decision makes my legs run.

If the 'mind' or 'spirit' can operate my legs, then they are, it seems, part of the same world as my legs.

This does not mean that the whole of existence is physical, any more than that it is purely spiritual or mental. We could say here that the whole of existence belongs to a category beyond this duality that we have invented. How to describe that category is still to be articulated, perhaps.

Consciousness

We have just spoken of the 'spirit' and the 'mind' as being perhaps interchangeable ideas. They are certainly both related to the idea of CONSCIOUSNESS or awareness.

We have said that we are conscious, or aware, of having a mind.

And, in Part One of this book, we have said that 'spiritual' experience involves a change in the form of consciousness, where we move into the realm of spiritual qualia.

Clearly, the notion of such consciousness, and, indeed, any consciousness, is central to this work.

To account, if we wish to, for 'spirituality' as a valid notion and spiritual experience as a valid experience, we must explore 'consciousness' itself as a part of the world.

Up to now, science, as we said earlier, has failed to account for 'consciousness,' how it occurs, and how it influences the physical world, simply because, we have said, it is a private, non-objective experience that cannot be directly observed through normal objective science.

If there is only one world, not two, we maybe should look to new thinking and perhaps a new sort of science to explore and account for awareness or consciousness and thus inform all our discussion of mind and spirituality.

It might be noted here that consciousness can be seen as having two modes: the passive and the active.

Awareness, to which we have frequently referred, can be thought of as passive consciousness, i.e. simply the experience of the qualia. The act of conscious decision-making is, perhaps, the active mode of consciousness. This second mode will be very important in our coming account of attempts at analysis.

Quantum Mechanics and Spirituality

Professor Roger Penrose, a recent Nobel laureate for Physics, and Stuart Hameroff, a distinguished anesthesiologist known for his studies of consciousness, have looked separately and then together at this. They have produced a number of publications and, together, edited an early book of academic papers, "Consciousness and the Universe"[18], which just might, if accepted with their other writings and other people's related writings, lay the ground for a new account of consciousness and, perhaps, spirituality. All these writers centre their thinking around the sub-atomic world of Quantum Mechanics and Heisenberg's Uncertainty principle, which we briefly outlined in part One of this work.

We will here put forward an interpretation of these writings, which might be seen as taking our understanding further.

No one can presently explain or describe spiritual experience in objective terms, but these writers and others have put forward a set of ideas which may make possible an account of the means whereby the world of consciousness exists, communicates, and, amazingly, in one interpretation, structures our universe, and all this in terms acceptable, importantly, to 21st Century "scientific" rationality.

We will look at the general thrust of these ideas in relation to consciousness and spirituality, and we may find that they account for our experiences of time, our awareness of the connectedness of all things, as well as our convictions about free will, choice, and morality.

The central theme of these ideas is that Quantum Mechanics operates within the brain, which, it is claimed, then produces modes of procedure involving UNCERTAINTY, which we might recognise as those of the mind.

Using Quantum Mechanics and, later, Relativity (the two great advances in 20th Century physics), these ideas attempt to give us an account of the mathematical and physical structures that underpin our deep experience of being conscious beings in a vast universe.

Observation and Experience

But before looking into that, we must make a distinction between objective observation on the one hand and experience on the other.

There is all the difference in the world between observing, for example, a violent storm (in the manner of a meteorologist) and experiencing a violent storm by being in it. In the latter case, one might become terrified, and one would certainly get wet.

The meteorologist, on the other hand, is distanced from the storm, safe and warm in the observatory.

But with the unfolding of Quantum Theory from the middle of the 20th Century came the surprise that, in the world of sub-atomic particles, the act of observation can radically alter what is observed, that the observer has a relationship with what is observed and, later, that this relationship may, perhaps, be a two-way phenomenon. Observation, in quantum mechanics, maybe a bit like experiencing a rainstorm in the rain.

This all links with the fundamental problem of studying consciousness, for such study is self-referential.

Studying consciousness is itself, an act of consciousness.

The studying of consciousness is a bit like being in a rainstorm; it is inseparable from the experience of consciousness, a bit like experiencing a rainstorm and getting wet.

So the question of consciousness is not an easy one, but let us look at this attempt, just mentioned, at an account of it which posits the clear uncertainties of quantum mechanics as a model of the uncertainties of the mind or spirit.

Quantum Mechanics

We should re-state some of the accepted principles of Quantum theory.

Quantum mechanics is a fundamental theory in science that refers to the motion and interaction of sub-atomic entities. The objects in this subatomic world, such as protons, electrons, photons, neutrons, gluons and quarks, do not obey the classical laws of physics, i.e., the laws that objects like sticks and stones obey in the ordinary larger-scale world.

In our earlier section on Modern Science, we outlined some of the differences.

We will not go into the mathematics and physics of all this. We will simply point to characteristics of Quantum Mechanics that are relevant to our current discussion.

    1)   In the sub-atomic quantum world, objects (like photons) have the characteristics of both what we call 'particles' and what we call 'waves' (wave-particle duality).

    2)   In addition, any object can exist in more than one state (e.g. wave or particle, or spinning in different ways) at the same time.

    3)   Amazingly, one particle can affect the state of another particle at a distance without an apparent limit of distance when there is, it seems, no connection between them.

    4)   And importantly, what can be accurately predicted or measured in any Quantum situation is very limited. This is the Uncertainty Principle. If, for example, a sub-atomic object can be seen as a particle or a wave, there is an irreducible uncertainty about its position at any moment. This is often interpreted as a matter of probability.

One cannot simultaneously know, for example, the position of an electron within an atom and its velocity/momentum. This degree of uncertainty means that the outcomes of Quantum operations are uncertain, involving a number of possibilities and that this uncertainty is a fundamental feature of such operations.

All this is largely accepted in the world of physics, and all of it has a scientific, evidential base.

It all leads to a certain unpredictability of outcomes in any quantum process.

The world of subatomic particles, the world of Quantum Mechanics, is, thus, strange beyond words to us and nothing like the everyday world in which we live or, indeed, the everyday world of early twentieth-century physics. Our normal language presents us with difficulties in even describing Quantum processes.

A New Theory of Consciousness?

So, how do (some) scientists apply all this to "consciousness"?

A lot is known about the operation of the brain, and, in particular, about the operation of NEURONS, which are specialized brain cells that transmit information between other cells, allowing the brain's operation.

In the theory of consciousness that we are discussing, it is proposed that internal to each neuron, there are structures in which a Quantum world exists, populated by sub-atomic objects (electrons, gluons, etc.) subject to all the strange rules of Quantum mechanics.

The Uncertainty Principle implies that the conclusion of a Quantum operation is uncertain and unpredictable. There may be any number of possible outcomes, all of which are 'real' possibilities, but there is no way of knowing which one WE will be left with. And this applies, thus, the theory says, to all the operations of such neurons.

Then, in some way, amid this uncertainty, a CHOICE of the outcome that we see is arrived at, which directs the neuron's operation.

With thousands or more neurons all operating in this way, the operation of the brain itself in directing our activity is, thus, in the overall picture, uncertain and unpredictable, just like (?) the mental processes we say are in the mind.

So, is this a model of how the mind exists in the brain?

Our mind's deliberations seem to be unpredictable and uncertain; this brain model is, it seems, exactly the same in this respect.

And what we may, indeed, call a CHOICE is made of the outcome of each Quantum operation, and the COMBINATION of many such outcomes leads to what we can call an overall CHOICE, causing the brain to initiate action.

In what may appear to be a fundamental insight central to this theory, it is proposed that these moments of CHOICE are moments of CONSCIOUSNESS. This is where, in the brain, consciousness is said to be.

The uncertainties of human thought and decision-making, it is said, are the uncertainties in brain operation resulting from Quantum operations within neurons.

Artificial Intelligence and Conscious Minds

The above is an attractive possible model of consciousness for the following reasons.

Many efforts have been made in mathematical physics to give an account of the "mind" just in terms of ordinary computer operations. Computers follow logical decision-making processes, and thus the end point of a computer operation is, in principle, predictable and determined if you know the start point and the logic involved.

This is why, perhaps, attempts to create A.I. models of the mind have failed and will continue to fail. The mind is not a computer; its operations and outcomes are not predictable or determined.

A.I. may be becoming more complex and, indeed, may be able, perhaps dangerously, to far surpass human brains in certain operations, leading to a possible loss of control by humans or its malevolent use. Predicting outcomes may become so complex that it is beyond any practical human attempt to do it. But it is still, in principle, predictable and determined.

The attraction of the Quantum model above is that while the outcomes of human mind operations are indeed uncertain and unpredictable, this is precisely the central characteristic of the Quantum model.

The mind is not a computer; it is an unpredictable entity. Quantum theorists seem to have given an account using Quantum theory, which fits the bill.

With recent developments of what are called "Quantum Computers," we seem to have something of vastly faster and greater(?), computer power, but still, such machines do just what classical computers do, but so fast that no classical computer can rival them, if they are reliable. Doubts about Quantum Computers remain in some quarters, however, principally because of the still obscure role of Quantum Uncertainty in such machines.

It is ironic that the very characteristic of Quantum mechanics which is at the centre of the Quantum theory of brain/mind, is the same characteristic that causes some doubt in some quarters about Quantum computing.

But, for our purposes, we must continue our investigation of the Quantum brain/mind theory to see if it fits our needs in terms of spirituality.

Evidence for the Quantum Mind Model

There is SOME evidence supporting this whole theory, but it is commonly accepted in the scientific world that supporting (or refuting) observation and experiment in relation to it is not possible, given current levels of technology. It is just not presently possible to carry out the necessary observational processes. Therefore, Such confirmation or refutation may have to wait for decades until sufficiently advanced technology has arrived. And such may never arrive.

In summary, despite this, the model produced undoubtedly involves the uncertainty of outcome and, thus, the unpredictability of what we may call choice. The model fits what we understand as the operation of a conscious mind; thus, may we see this as a model of the way the mind works, as a possible description of the mind?

Freewill and Morality?

This model has some interesting corollaries. The idea of what is called 'choice' in this model leads some to assert that here is the origin of our belief in free will and morality, for each, by definition, involves choice. If we experience making choices, we cannot, perhaps, escape assuming that we have free will. If we experience making choices of various actions, then maybe that is how we come to the idea that one choice is 'better' than another, leading to ideas of 'good' and 'bad' choices. Then we can develop ideas about 'good' and 'bad' in themselves and seek, in our lives, perception about the nature of the difference. The idea of morality is born (?).

Implications for our view of the universe

The tremendously important central process of combining these many neuron outcomes (e.g., when deciding something) is asserted by the theorists who advocate it to be a QUANTUM-GRAVITY process, which also relates to the fundamentals of space/time geometry and Relativity.

Relativity is a theory about the universe on a grand scale. Perhaps, some say, there is, thus, a connection between brain processes, as described here, and the fine-scale structure of the universe.

In support of this assertion, certain measurements of magnetic force fields in the brain appear, surprisingly, to be at a similar scale to those in cosmological studies.

This quantum-gravity proposal takes quantum mechanics into areas not yet fully developed. It suggests a need for a 'theory of everything', combining Quantum Mechanics and Relativity, to understand the universe and, indeed, some claim, consciousness.

Consciousness and the Cosmos

Astonishingly, this proposal suggests, as above, possible operational connections between consciousness and the cosmos. For what we are now, perhaps, seeing, according to this theory, as the Quantum structures which operate the mind are the very structures of the material of which all the stuff of the universe is made.

Protons, electrons, neutrons, photons, muons, quarks, and any other sub-atomic entities yet to be discovered are the material of which all matter and energy are made. So, it is suggested that the whole universe is constructed of the same stuff as our minds and consciousnesses. The entities that bring about consciousness interact with each other in quantum ways. They affect each other at a distance, and instantaneously, that is, they communicate with each other. Perhaps the same processes can then be ascribed to all matter, say some theorists, since matter is made of the same sorts of stuff. So, the universe can be seen as consisting of structures and patterns of quantum entities, all interacting through quantum processes, including action at a distance and embracing uncertainty.

If the Quantum/Relativity proposal is accepted, then the whole universe might also be seen to be behaving, in some ways, astonishingly like a mind or, in my view, a spirit.

And everything in it, either individually or collectively!

Not only every human being but every animal and every plant are part of this.

Not only every living thing, but every rock, every liquid, every gas, every planet, every star, every galaxy, and everything in intergalactic space is part of this.

So, according to all this, the whole of the universe and everything in it would have some of the characteristics of mind, i.e. all of existence, indeed, is, it seems, an interacting, intercommunicating, interconnected vast entity, with some of the characteristics of a mind. And we are just a small part of this.

Wow! This all seems similar to the conclusions one may come to, through spiritual practice, of a universe where one senses unity and, indeed, an eternal, over-arching unity with which one may be in communion.

So, if all this Quantum stuff is accepted, can we find here the intellectual space in which to talk, in 'scientific terms' of landscapes speaking to us, of feeling love for all living things, for a feeling of love and peace coming from the mere stones of which a cathedral is made, or the 'glory of God' shining through the very floorboards of a Quaker Meeting House?

Well, can we?

We appear to have an account, not of our spiritual experience itself, but of how our deepest spiritual experience can arise.

A Universal Self?

There are, indeed, implications for the notion of 'self,' for if our brains, our minds, and our spirits (our individual 'selves) are part of one unified, integrated, inter-communicating whole, which is, in fact, the universe, then, perhaps, we may say that we are part of a universal 'Self'.

We may, as some indeed do, experience that oneness where our own individual 'self' is dissolved in the universal 'Self' through meditation or worship.

We might also say that when we do experience that unity, the experience is, in fact, best articulated and described as LOVE.

Further Possibilities

We could go further, as some have done, and follow the logic of the quantum 'choice' of outcomes as an argument for a multiverse, where each POSSIBLE outcome to a quantum process actually does occur and each creates another possible universe.

We could also explore the theory that each quantum entity (e.g. an electron) has a corresponding anti-entity (e.g. a positron), leading into the whole idea of anti-matter. Positrons are not only known to exist, but are actually used in PET medical scans. PET means Positron Emission Tomography.

But we do not need any of this at present.

The Quantum/Relativity account itself gives us enough to continue, IF we wish to accept it.

We have, perhaps, the basis for a valid dialogue about the 'self', and the universal 'Self'. Perhaps, some may think, spiritual awareness of "the silence of eternity interpreted by love" can spring out of this awareness of the universe as the Self.

Science and Spirituality???

However, scientific observation and theorising are very different from the subjective experience of the spirituality of all things.

Suppose the Quantum/Relativity theory of the mind gains support and acceptance within the scientific community. In that case, it may be the basis of that necessary 21st Century dialogue about the nature of the universe and man's place in it as a conscious organism. It may become a way, so sorely needed, of speaking with 21st Century man about the fundamental questions of existence and the spiritual nature of things.

But the Quantum/relativity account still fails, crucially, to penetrate subjective experience.

We must go back to our distinction between observation and experience. We may have a proposal for a theoretical model of the mechanics of the mind loosely based on observation, but the deep experience of spirituality is still beyond such observation.

In the same way that we know the mechanics of eyesight, from the wavelengths of light entering the eye to the operation of the optic nerve in making a connection to the brain, but have no access to your EXPERIENCE of the colour blue, we may think we have a possible theory of how consciousness arises in the brain (via Quantum/Relativity), but this would give no access to actual conscious experience, including the experience of spiritual insight.

So we have here a possible, partly developed theory of how 'mind' or 'consciousness' arises in the world of flesh, but it remains the case that our individual subjective experiences of consciousness remain out of the reach of objective science.

Indeed, the scientific writings in this area take no account, as far as I can see, of what we saw earlier as the central, vital base of spirituality: private, individual, subjective experience and the change in the FORM of consciousness that allows experience leading to spiritual conviction.

Spirituality is not a matter of physics, even advanced Quantum Physics. It is a matter of the private, subjective experience found when the form of consciousness is changed in a way at the heart of our account of things and well-known to those who have experienced it.

William James, author of "The Varieties of Religious Experience"[19], and the foremost and most influential writer and thinker in this area over a hundred years or more ago, refers specifically to this. He argues that 'consciousness' is not the core; it is what consciousness EXPERIENCES that is the central matter. So, for us, the experience of the change in the form of consciousness is the basic notion.

In fact, James suggests that we should stop talking about 'consciousness' and simply look at 'experience' instead. For James, experience is the core.

In the end, objective science, even a new objective science, cannot account for personal, private, subjective experience, whether it be of the colour blue, the beauty of a work of art, or the transcendent spirituality of things.

It is, indeed, tempting for some to see an account of consciousness, like the one under discussion, as a possible answer to the question of subjective experience, but such a model can still only deal with the objective. It may be able to talk about observable and mathematical mechanisms related to consciousness, but it cannot enter the subjective world of the mind/spirit and its experience.

And it is this private, subjective experience that lies at the heart of our analysis.

Stories and Models

In the first part of this work, "The Allegory of God," we said that all the stories told by the traditional faiths were allegories about the spiritual nature of things. They existed to enable humans to talk and think about the spirituality they experienced; they sometimes led people into a deeper spirituality beyond the stories, but, of course, they also often, or even usually, led people astray from spirituality because the stories were not the core experiential insight, and they often led to very different interpretations, causing much discord.

It is, perhaps, also the case that the stories told by any objective science will also, in failing to enter the subjective, be open to different interpretations of the subjective experience.

Indeed, there are parallels between the stories told by science and those told by the traditional faiths. They are both attempts to understand the world, the universe, and ourselves. In science, what is constructed is not labelled 'stories'. Rather, they are called 'models'. What our observation of the universe and maths allow us to construct is the 'model' of the universe which best fits, and which we best see as our view of the cosmos. This is the equivalent, in some ways, of the tales told by theologians.

They are both ways of thinking/talking about the big questions of our existence. They are different ways in which humans have tried just to make sense of our world.

The stories of science, like those of the religions, have provided a space within which dialogue, discussion, or argument about existence can proceed.

Scientific discourse has proceeded very successfully in its terms, i.e., those of the objective, the observable universe., though sometimes leading to conflict and suffering (experiments on humans, better ways of killing people, nuclear weapons, climate change).

In some ways, in their own terms, religious discourse has also proceeded successfully, though often also leading to conflict and suffering (religious wars, persecutions, negation of much human fulfilment).

But, leaving, as we must, all stories and models behind, we, in the end, of course, come back to our central interest; the subjective experience of the spiritual nature of things.

This remains beyond objective investigation of any kind.

It seems we are each alone in our subjective experiential world of spirituality.

Communion

But, of course, that is not the case.

When people come together in meditation, prayer, or worship, the spiritual experience can become something shared so that we have what we might call an inter-subjective experience of the transcendent, the holy, and the divine. We have a word for this: COMMUNION.

This happens in many religious worship settings. In mosques, gurdwaras, temples, churches, chapels, and in the open air, as well as in people's houses, with people coming together in reverent and loving openness to the transcendent, finding that the experience of communion is available, and often, actual. When all the paraphernalia of ritual, creed, and hierarchy is stripped away, the possibility of communion remains.

It doesn't always happen, and then people are left with whatever the cultural clothing of their faith provides.

But the experience of communion is the central and essential core: communion with each other's spirit and with the loving and transcendent presence of the eternal Self.

This presence is the very ground of our being and the basis of all things.

So, in the end, we indeed place science, even Quantum science, on one side and come back to the beginning: our experience of the spiritual nature of all things.

This experience or perception is enough. It is as certain as our perception of colour, sound and all the qualia of our experience.

It is self-evident and undeniable.

Time and Eternity

General Relativity, which Quantum theorists of 'mind' use in their account of the combinations of neuron quantum outcomes, leads to the consideration of relativist accounts of 'time'.

Our normal view of time is of something moving ever forward at a regular rate. It is measured by clocks of ever-increasing accuracy.

"Time, like an ever-rolling stream, bears all its sons away."

But, for Albert Einstein, time is a relativistic thing. It is one of the four dimensions of Space/Time with which Relativity deals. The rate at which it 'flows' varies relative to how fast you are moving and to how close you may be to other bodies, e.g., the Earth. So, the rate is different for different objects. Time passes at a different rate, for example, for Earth's satellites from the rate at which it passes on the Earth's surface.

This is evidenced by the most practical of considerations.

It is only the application of relativity Theory that permits the accurate location of cars on roads by "satnav" satellites. If Relativity was not taken into account, your sat nav would not be able to position you, perhaps, at better than up to a mile from where you are because the two clocks (in satellite and in-car) are seeing different rates of time passing (leading to mistakes in calculations). Whereas, as we know, they can locate you to within yards or, perhaps, feet, and this is because they take into account the different relativistic time rates when calculating your position.

So, time passes at different rates in different circumstances.

Some aspects of time appear to be an illusion, according to remarks of Einstein. The future and the past are, he says, illusions, albeit persistent ones. We only have access to the present moment, indeed. The past is merely a present memory, existing only in your mind. Future time is only in your imagination.

So, what price is "eternity"?

The things that are described in religious texts as in eternity include various versions of bliss: Nirvana, the Kingdom of heaven, paradise, and so on. They are pictured as worlds to which, if we are lucky or virtuous, we go after death, i.e., in the future, and they are everlasting.

But remember the amazing reported words of Jesus of Nazareth: "The Kingdom of Heaven is within you". If it is within you, then it is in this present moment. It is now, or at least, it is available now. Eternity is, therefore, not just something stretching out into time without end. It is with you; it is outside any idea of the flow of time or any idea of time itself. Eternity is in this moment. Heaven, Paradise and Nirvana are here and now, as possibilities.

This accords with our account of the commonly experienced transformation of consciousness in worship or meditation, when we seem to perceive all space and all time, that is, we seem to have a perception of eternity.

In some sense, it is all outside of time, as we commonly imagine time.

The notion of "life after death" or "everlasting life in the next world" doesn't arise because our existence is in the Now, where the Kingdom of Heaven (or its equivalent or alternative) is. Now is the eternal moment.

Therefore, do not worry about where you go after death; you are already there, perhaps, in this eternal moment!

And this is not always a fortunate position to be in. Many sad souls experience what can only be called "Hell" (the apparent alternative!) in the present moment. Helping people in this position is, for many, a life-long piece of work that advances "The Kingdom of Heaven."

Your place in the universe is established by your presence now and the life you lead. And your place in the history of the universe, in space/time, is indestructible in some way.

We will, perhaps, never understand the way this occurs.

"There are more things in heaven and earth…. than are dreamt of in your philosophy."[20] There is much beyond any words we may put together.

Be at peace. After everything is said, the experience of a glimpse of eternity is enough.

Conclusions

"Where mercy, love, and pity dwell, there God is dwelling too."[21]

William Blake

With our undeniable experience of transformed consciousness and our possible understanding of how religious language works, we can move to a possible developing understanding of those existential questions that have haunted humankind since conscious experience dawned.

But we are on a journey in which our perception of things changes and develops throughout our lives. The journey, I think, never ends. And that's fine. In fact, the journey continues even now and into what we call the future. The rest of each of our lives may bring new perceptions and new insights to each of us. And that's fine, too!

I sometimes call the overall view here "Reverent Humanism", because I take the humanist view to be that all understanding comes from experience, and I have emphasised that everything we have said here is based on experience, including the experience of a transformed consciousness giving us a sense of the eternal, the divine, the universal.

We can clothe it in traditional language if we wish, as long as we recognise the allegorical nature of that language.

So I am happy with people talking about God, or Nirvana, or redemption. Whatever they speak of is simply a way of referring to the eternal.

But do not be so tied to the allegorical language that it leads you into conflict with others, or leads you through its limitations or prohibitions into denying some of the fulfilments that human life offers.

Live happily with your fellow humans, in tolerance, kindness, pity, mercy, and love.

See the eternal in all its different cultural manifestations, but hold on to the eternal, the universal, and you will be at peace with life and the universe.

You may experience that oneness with all people and all things that is a glimpse of the divine.

Maybe you are there already.

References

1) **Milford Q. Sibley** (1979). *Quaker Mysticism: Its Context and Implications.* Quaker Universalist Fellowship. See: https://universalistfriends.org/pdf/quf2000a.pdf

2) *Advices and Queries* (2013). The Yearly Meeting of the Religious Society of Friends (Quakers) in Britain. Para. 1.02, No. 1.

3) *Philippians* 4 v.7.

4) The Alister Hardy Trust, Archives at University of Wales, Trinity St David, Lampeter.

See http://www.uwtsd.ac.uk/library/alister-hardy-religious-experience-research-centre/

5) See, e.g. http://www.beliefnet.com/faiths/hinduism/2009/07/gandhi-quotes.aspx

6) **C.S.Lewis** (1942). *The Screwtape Letters.* The Centenary Press.

7) See, e.g. http://bigthink.com/scotty-hendricks/what-nietzsche-really-meant-by-god-is-dead

8) *1 John* 4 vv. 8-9

9) Pierre Laplace, mathematician and scientist, is reputed to have replied to Napoleon's question of why he had made no mention of God in his new book: "Je n'avais pas besoin de cette hypothèse-là".

10) See Reference 4.

11) Quoted in *The Daily Telegraph* Science News 'ten best quotes' on 30/3/2012. It is derived from Einstein's remark that "the distinction between past, present and future is only a stubbornly *persistent illusion"*. *(See **A. Calaprice** (2000). The Expanded Quotable Einstein. Princeton UP.)*

12) See: https://www.eng.famu.fsu.edu/~dommelen/quantum/style_a/botline.html

13) idem

14) **Jocelyn Bell Burnell** (2013). *A Quaker Astronomer Reflects*. The James Backhouse Lectures, Book 23.

15) **Einstein** in a letter to Hans Muehsam (1954). *Einstein Archive* 38-434.

16) **Albert Einstein** (1931). *Einstein on Cosmic Religion with Other Opinions and Aphorisms.* Re-published by Dover Publications Inc., New York, 2009.

17) **Ludwig Wittgenstein** (1921). *Tractatus Logico-Philosophicus.* Many English translations of this major philosophical work are available.

18) **Roger Penrose, Stuart Hameroff, and Subhash Kak** (2009). *Conciousness and the Universe* , Chapter One. Published by Cosmology Science publishers, Cambridge, Mass., USA.

19) **William James** (1902) *The Varieties of Religious Experience.* Longmans, Green, and Co.

20) **William Shakespeare.** *HAMLET,* Act One, Scene V, " There are more things in Heaven and earth, Horatio, than are dreamt of in your Philosophy".

21) **Willam Blake** (1789) *The Divine Image, in Songs of Innocence.*

www.ingramcontent.com/pod-product-compliance
Lightning Source LLC
Chambersburg PA
CBHW050033040726
47599CB00015B/1660